Your Gift

I wanted to show my appreciation that you ....y work so I've put together a free gift for you.

http://bonusfreebook.org/

Just visit the link above to download it now.

I know you will love this gift.

If you like this book, you can see and buy my other books on this link:

ALL BOOKS MAYA CLARK HERE

Thank you for attention!

With love,

Maya Clark

Table of Contents

Introduction

As for giving a simple definition for this classic Mexican dish, we can say that they are corn tortillas made with flour and you can fold or wrap them around different kind of fillings. The main toppings that were used for tortillas were cilantro and cebollita, but nowadays they were slowly replaced with spicy salsa sauces, squeezed lime, guac or other extra spicy sauces. We are going to present you everything that you must know about this most delicious snack that is loved by so many people around the world.

The origins of the tacos still remain unclear, but many researchers pretend that comes from the Nahuatl word "Flacco" (in the middle), which was used by the Mexican miners for "plug". Another Spanish proof is that the food is dating from the people that left in the Valley of Mexico, and the Spanish conquistadors have served tacos during their expeditions.

The oldest tacos that were recorded are mentioned in the Valley of Mexico and were served with some small fish. Nowadays the typical tacos are made with different kind of meats, starting from the fruity tacos al pastor, which are made with slices of pork meat infused with some pineapple juice and barbacoa, up to chorizo tacos, tacos de "Pescado" (fish) or de camaron (prawn). The camaron tacos can be found on the Mexican coastline. Usually, the prawn versions are lighter than the ones with greasy meat and mostly are topped with Pico de Gallo, lettuce, tomatoes and avocado.

While in the world the tacos are cooked different, the traditional ones feature a tender tortilla and a greasy inner of meats such as beef, chicken or others. You might also find different kinds of tacos that are popular in Mexico that are more delicious than expected.

They can be found on almost every street food vendor in Mexico cities, especially in highly populated places or small villages. If you prefer to eat a more sophisticated version of tacos, you can check out the indoor markets which serve the best tacos in the city. If you are planning a trip to Mexico City you have to visit the most popular restaurant in this town, named El Fogoncito, which it's highly recommended by any local experts in tacos.

In this book, we are going to present you a couple of taco recipes that are popular in the Mexico City region and inspired by local citizens or restaurants. We highly recommend you use as much as possible the pointed ingredients, and Mexican original sauces for a better taste. You will find easy to cook these taco recipes and you can eat them as a snack together with your friends or family

Chapter 1 –
Chicken and Turkey

Slow Cooker Chicken Tacos

Cooking time: 8 hours 15 minutes

Portions: 8 persons

Ingredients:

- 1 lb chicken breasts
- 1 pack taco seasoning
- 1 jar salsa
- 2-3 tomatoes
- Cheddar cheese

Directions:

1. Take a medium crock pot and cook the chicken meat for about 8 hours over low heat. Before serving it on tortillas, shred it and add the rest of the ingredients and seasonings.

Nutrition Facts:

1 portion: 91.3 calories, 3.2 g fat, 33.1 mg cholesterol, 362.9 mg sodium, 4.4 g carbs, 1.1 g dietary fiber, 12.8 g protein.

Quick and Easy Ground Turkey Tacos

Cooking time: 35 minutes

Portions: 8 persons

Ingredients:

- 1 pound ground turkey
- taco seasonings
- 1 cup shredded cheese
- $\frac{3}{4}$ cup water
- 1 can diced tomatoes with basil, oregano, and garlic
- 1 can black beans
- low carb tortillas & lettuce (optional)

Directions:

1. Into a medium skillet start frying the turkey meat until it gets brown. Add the water, diced tomatoes and beans, simmering until they get consistent. Spoon the mixture over each tortilla, adding lettuce and shredded cheese.

Nutrition Facts:

1 portion: 242.7 calories, 7.9 g fat, 44.0 mg cholesterol, 835.8 mg sodium, 25.1 g carbs, 10.8 g dietary fiber, 17.7 g protein.

Slow Cooker Cilantro Lime Chicken Tacos

Cooking time: 10 minutes

Portions: 6 persons

Ingredients:

- 1 lb chicken breasts
- 1 jar salsa
- 3 tbsp. fresh cilantro
- 1 pack Taco seasoning
- 1 Lime (juice)
- 6 whole wheat Tortillas

Directions:

1. Place the chicken meat, taco seasoning, cilantro, lime juice and salsa into a medium slow cooker; cooking for 8-10 hours over low heat (you can do this overnight).
2. When done, shred the meat and place it over your tortillas, adding the toppings to taste (olives, lettuce, onions & other sauces).

Nutrition Facts:

1 portion: 212.2 calories, 2.3 g fat, 21.8 mg cholesterol, 793.7 mg sodium, 31.8 g carbs, 2.6 g dietary fiber, 13.2 g protein.

Chicken Tacos with Homemade Salsa

Cooking time: 15 minutes
Portions: 2 persons
Ingredients:

Spicy Meat:
- 1 chicken breast (cubed)
- 1 garlic clove
- $\frac{1}{2}$ tomato
- $\frac{1}{2}$ tsp. onion & chili powder
- $\frac{1}{2}$ tsp. cuminutes & paprika
- $\frac{1}{2}$ lime (juice)

Salsa:
- $\frac{1}{4}$ cup diced onion
- $\frac{1}{2}$ diced tomato
- 1 pinch of salt
- $\frac{1}{4}$ cup fresh cilantro
- $\frac{1}{2}$ lime juice
- $\frac{1}{2}$ diced avocado
- $\frac{1}{2}$ small Jalapeño pepper

Other:
- 4 corn tortillas
- $\frac{1}{4}$ cup mozzarella cheese
- $\frac{1}{2}$ cup lettuce (shredded)

Directions:

1. Take a medium skillet, add the chicken, spices, garlic and lime juice, cooking everything until just done. Pour the diced tomatoes over the fried chicken.
2. Meanwhile, start mixing the ingredients for salsa sauce. Heat each corn tortilla, add the chicken mixture, lettuce, salsa sauce, and mozzarella.

Nutrition Facts:

1 portion: 301.6 calories, 9.4 g fat, 41.2 mg cholesterol, 390.8 mg sodium, 36.1 g carbs, 7.2 g dietary fiber, 23.2 g protein.

Lime Chicken Soft Tacos

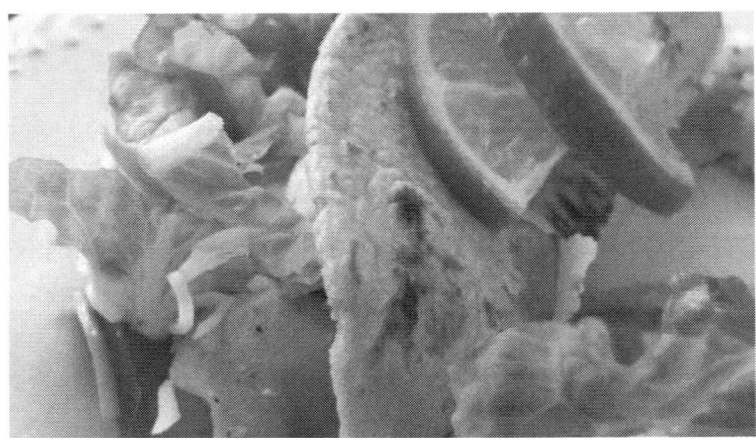

Cooking time: 40 minutes
Portions: 10 persons

Ingredients:

- 1 ½ lbs. breast meat (cubed)
- 10 Fajita size tortillas
- ¼ cup red wine vinegar
- ¼ cup salsa sauce
- ½ lime juice
- 1 tsp. splenda
- ¼ cup Monterey Jack cheese (shredded)
- ½ tsp. salt & ground black pepper
- 1 diced tomato
- ½ cup lettuce (shredded)
- 2 green onions & garlic cloves
- 1 tsp. dried oregano

Directions:

1. In a medium saucepan, sauté the chicken breast over medium heat for about 15 minutes. Add some lime juice, green onion, vinegar, oregano and other seasonings, simmering everything well for 5 more minutes.
2. Heat up each fajita tortilla into a large skillet over medium heat on each side. Make each tortilla, adding the chicken meat mixture, lettuce, salsa sauce, tomatoes and shredded cheese.

Nutrition Facts:

1 portion: 163.9 calories, 2.4 g fat, 33.2 mg cholesterol, 451.7 mg sodium, 14.0 g carbs, 7.3 g dietary fiber, 17.6 g protein.

Tex Mex Chicken Tacos

Cooking time: 2 hours 10 minutes
Portions: 4 persons
Ingredients:

- 8 corn tortillas
- 1 lb. chicken breast (pieces)
- $\frac{1}{2}$ cup sour cream
- $\frac{1}{2}$ cup orange juice
- 1 tsp. cornstarch
- $\frac{1}{4}$ cup fresh cilantro
- 1 cup frozen whole kernel corn
- 1 tsp. lime peel
- 1 jalapeno pepper
- 1 medium sweet red pepper
- 3 garlic cloves
- 2 tsp. olive oil
- $\frac{1}{4}$ tsp. salt and black pepper

Directions:

1. Place the chicken meat and other marinade ingredients into a plastic bag and place it into the fridge for 1-2 hours. When it's well marinated, drain it and cook it into a medium frying pan, until crispy and tender. Add the sweet peppers, some marinade and cornstarch and cook everything for 2 minutes more.
2. Heat up each tortilla in your microwave for 40 seconds, divide the chicken among them, and add some sour cream, lettuce, onions, and seasonings.

Nutrition Facts:

1 portion: 307.1 calories, 8.8 g fat, 61.3 mg cholesterol, 187.5 mg sodium, 34.6 g carbs, 4.0 g dietary fiber, 25.4 g protein.

Chicken Tacos on Hard Shells & Refried Beans

Cooking time: 60 minutes
Portions: 5 persons

Ingredients:

- 1 cup shredded Mexican cheese
- 5 corn tacos
- 1 lb. chicken meat
- 1 pack taco seasonings
- 1 cup chopped onions & tomatoes
- $\frac{3}{4}$ cup water & 1 can refried beans
- 3 oz. Spinach leaves
- $\frac{1}{2}$ cup salsa sauce

Directions:

1. Start cutting the chicken meat and onions into small pieces, then cook them into a medium skillet over medium heat for 2-3 minutes. Add the spinach leaves, water and seasonings, bring everything to a boil.
2. Warm up each corn tortilla in a microwave oven, add the chicken mixture, some more spinach leaves, tomatoes, refried beans, salsa sauce, cheese and some seasonings.

Nutrition Facts:

1 portion: 448.7 calories, 11.2 g fat, 91.3 mg cholesterol, 1,293.5 mg sodium, 35.9 g carbs, 7.7 g dietary fiber, 44.9 g protein.

Apple and Onion Chicken Soft Tacos

Cooking time: 25 minutes
Portions: 4 persons

Ingredients:

- 6 Flour tortillas
- 2 chicken breasts (cubes)
- 1 tbsp. butter
- 1 garlic clove
- ½ Tsp. ground nutmeg & black pepper
- 2 cups sliced apples & 1 cup sliced onion
- 4 tbsp. mango salsa
- 1 tbsp. olive oil

Directions:

1. Over medium heat, heat some butter into a medium frying pan. Add the apples and onions, cooking them until they get browned. Take out the apples and onions, and cook the cubed chicken breasts until cooked through. Transfer the onions and apples, minced garlic and seasonings. Top each tortilla with the mixture and some mango salsa.

Nutrition Facts:

1 portion: 484.1 calories, 13.0 g fat, 76.4 mg cholesterol, 499.5 mg sodium, 54.8 g carbs, 5.4 g dietary fiber, 34.1 g protein.

Fajita Chicken Tacos

Cooking time: 25 minutes
Portions: 1 person

Ingredients:

- 1 lb. Chicken Meat
- 3 corn tortillas
- $\frac{1}{4}$ can cheddar cheese
- 1 tsp. fajita seasoning
- $\frac{1}{4}$ can tomatoes
- $\frac{1}{4}$ lettuce
- 1 tbsp. salsa-mild

Directions:

1. Cook the chunk, chicken, and fajita seasonings. In a medium pan, warm up each corn tortilla, until they get crispy. Place 1 teaspoon of salsa sauce over each tortilla, add the chicken and other vegetables.

Nutrition Facts:

1 portion: 436.8 calories, 13.0 g fat, 95.2 mg cholesterol, 551.6 mg sodium, 41.3 g carbs, 6.1 g dietary fiber, 38.9 g protein.

Fiesta Chicken Tacos

Cooking time: ~~20 minutes~~ 6-8 hours
Portions: 10 persons

Ingredients:

- 1 ½ lb. chicken breast
- ½ tbsp. onion & garlic powder
- 1 can nacho cheese soup
- 1 pack taco seasoning
- 6 tbsp. green chili sauce
- 4 tbsp. salsa

Directions:

1. Take a crockpot and add the chicken breast. In a medium bowl, mix the other ingredients and then pour them over the chicken. Set the cooking time to 6-8 hours over low heat. Shred the chicken using a small knife.

Nutrition Facts:

1 portion: 120.7 calories, 3.6 g fat, 43.1 mg cholesterol, 578.6 mg sodium, 6.1 g carbs, 0.8 g dietary fiber, 14.7 g protein.

Chapter 2 – Beef, pork, and lamb

Beef Tacos

Cooking time: 20 minutes
Portions: 8 persons

Ingredients:

- ½ lb. lean ground beef
- 8 whole wheat tortillas
- 1 pack taco seasoning
- Shredded romaine lettuce & 2 large tomatoes
- ¾ cup water
- 2 cups shredded cheddar cheese

Directions:

1. Into a medium pan add some water, ground beef, and taco seasoning, then bring everything to a boil. Heat up the tacos on both sides according to the package directions, then top with the meat, veggies, and sauce.

Nutrition Facts:

1 portion: 351.2 calories, 22.5 g fat, 69.4 mg cholesterol, 284.9 mg sodium, 12.7 g carbs, 1.6 g dietary fiber, 23.0 g protein.

Beef Wild Mushroom, Steak, and Poblano Tacos

Cooking time: 20 minutes
Portions: 6 persons

Ingredients:

- 1 tbsp. olive oil
- 12 corn tortillas
- 1 lb. beef steak
- 12 tbsp. salsa sauce & $\frac{1}{2}$ tsp. coriander
- $\frac{1}{2}$ tsp. salt & black pepper
- 2 cups raw onion & 1 cup minutesced garlic
- $\frac{3}{4}$ cup Mexican cheese and 1 Poblano pepper
- 2 cups wild mushrooms

Directions:

1. Start browning the steak beef meat into an oiled medium pan, together with salt and pepper seasonings. After cooking for 5 minutes on both sides, take out   the steaks and set them aside. Add the remaining ingredients into the pan and sauté them for 5 minutes.
2. Serve the warm tortillas topped with the mushroom mixture, sliced steak meat, salsa sauce and shredded Mexican cheese.

Nutrition Facts:

1 portion: 285.6 calories, 14.1 g fat, 57.8 mg cholesterol, 478.7 mg sodium, 18.9 g carbs, 3.0 g dietary fiber, 19.5 g protein.

Shredded Pork Tacos

Cooking time: 35 minutes
Portions: 12 persons

Ingredients:

- ½ pound pork roast
- 12 soft homemade tacos
- 1 cup sliced onions
- ½ cup chopped tomatoes & 1 avocado
- 1 can tomatoes & 2-3 jalapeno chiles
- ½ cup sour cream sauce
- 1 ancho chili & 1 cup water
- 1 cup shredded lettuce
- ½ tsp. salt & pepper
- 1 cup shredded cheddar cheese

Directions:

1. Take a large saucepan and add the chopped pork meat, vegetables, water and seasonings, cooking for 20 minutes stirring occasionally. Remove the vegetables and chicken meat from the cooking liquid and shred them into small pieces.
2. Assemble the homemade tortillas with lettuce, pork meat, vegetables, sour cream sauce, shredded cheese, diced tomatoes, and avocados.

Nutrition Facts:

1 portion: 394.7 calories, 21.5 g fat, 58.5 mg cholesterol, 652.3 mg sodium, 29.4 g carbs, 2.2 g dietary fiber, 22.2 g protein.

Low Fat Beef & Bean Tacos

Cooking time: 20 minutes

Portions: 4 persons

Ingredients:

- 1 lb. ground beef
- refried beans
- 8 taco shells & taco seasoning
- 1 sweet onion
- salsa sauce
- shredded cheddar cheese
- 1 sliced avocado
- sour cream

Directions:

1. Start cooking the beef into an oiled pan and add the beans and seasonings. Place the tacos onto a plate and add the meat mixture, salsa sauce, sour cream, sliced avocado and shredded cheddar cheese.

Nutrition Facts:

1 portion: 541.1 calories, 19.9 g fat, 74.2 mg cholesterol, 1,423.5 mg sodium, 52.9 g carbs, 11.2 g dietary fiber, 43.3 g protein.

Taco Truck Tacos

Cooking time: 25 minutes
Portions: 4 persons

Ingredients:

- 1.5 lbs. pork shoulder (shredded)
- 1-2 Limes
- 12 corn tortillas
- 1 bunch cilantro
- ½ cup chopped onions
- Radishes, avocado & fresh Tomatoes

Directions:

1. Into a medium pan start browning the meat which was previously seasoned with cumin, salt, and pepper. When done, warm the tortillas over both sides and top them with the meat, onions, avocado, tomatoes and some lime juice.

Nutrition Facts:

1 portion: 371.9 calories, 16.7 g fat, 47.2 mg cholesterol, 98.9 mg sodium, 41.8 g carbs, 7.8 g dietary fiber, 17.7 g protein.

Sneaky Tacos

Cooking time: 25 minutes

Portions: 16 persons

Ingredients:

- 1 1/2 lbs. lean ground beef
- 8 whole corn tortillas
- 1 pack taco seasoning
- 1 jar salsa sauce
- 2 cups grated cheddar cheese

Directions:

1. In an oiled frying pan slowly brown the ground beef, add the salsa sauce and mix well, then drain the meat. Warm up each tortilla and add the meat mixture, seasonings, add some salsa sauce and cheddar cheese.

Nutrition Facts:

1 portion: 70.5 calories, 3.4 g fat, 17.2 mg cholesterol, 442.8 mg sodium, 4.6 g carbs, 0.3 g dietary fiber, 4.7 g protein.

BBQ beef tacos

Cooking time: 35 minutes
Portions: 8 persons

Ingredients:

- 1 lb. lean ground beef (or turkey)
- ½ cup Mexican shredded cheese
- 1 cutted onion & red pepper
- 8 whole wheat tortillas
- ½ cup barbecue sauce
- 1 diced tomato

Directions:

1. Start cooking the beef meat, onions and peppers in a medium oiled skillet until well done, stirring occasionally. Add the sauce and cook everything for 2 minutes. Pour the meat mixture over each tortilla and top with cheese and tomatoes before serving.

Nutrition Facts:

1 portion: 259.7 calories, 11.0 g fat, 47.8 mg cholesterol, 528.6 mg sodium, 27.6 g carbs, 4.8 g dietary fiber, 17.4 g protein.

Tacos De Barbacoa

Cooking time: 5 hours 20 minutes
Portions: 20 persons
Ingredients:

- 4 pounds beef meat
- $\frac{1}{4}$ cup cider vinegar
- 20 corn tortillas
- 3 tbsp. lime juice
- $\frac{3}{4}$ cup chicken broth
- 3-5 canned chipotle chiles
- 2 tbsp. vegetable oil & 3 bay leaves
- 4 garlic cloves & cuminutes
- 3 tsp. Mexican oregano
- 1 $\frac{1}{2}$ tsp. salt & ground black pepper
- $\frac{1}{2}$ tsp. ground cloves
- onion, cilantro and lime wedges (chopped)

Directions:

1. Mix into a medium bowl the lime juice, garlic cloves, cider vinegar and other seasonings, until they get smooth like a paste. Take the meat and cook it into an oiled skillet for 5 minutes, over both sides. Add the mixture from the bowl over the meat and keep stirring well.
2. After 10 more minutes, while the ingredients were simmering, add the mixture into the preheated oven. Cook for about 4-5 hours. Serve the corn tortillas with the oven mixture, onions, cilantro, lime wedges and other seasonings.

Nutrition Facts:

1 portion: 142.3 calories, 5.4 g fat, 53.2 mg cholesterol, 301.9 mg sodium, 1.5 g carbs, 0.6 g dietary fiber, 22.0 g protein.

Crispy Tacos

Cooking time: 30 minutes
Portions: 7 persons

Ingredients:

- 1 lb. ground beef
- 21 taco shells
- 2 tbsp. taco sauce
- 1 can Taco Bell re-fried beans
- 1-2 cups of shredded lettuce
- 1 tsp. chili seasoning mix
- 1.5 cups shredded cheese

Directions:

1. Start heating up your oven to 325 degrees Celsius and then cook the ground beef into a medium frying pan, until it gets finely browned. Add 2 tbsp. of sauce, seasonings and the re-fried beans, cooking until well warmed through.
2. Meanwhile, warm each tortilla into the oven for a few minutes, and then assemble with lettuce, sauce, meat mixture and some shredded cheese.

Nutrition Facts:

1 portion: 404.2 calories, 19.7 g fat, 62.1 mg cholesterol, 744.0 mg sodium, 30.9 g carbs, 3.5 g dietary fiber, 24.3 g protein.

Carne Asada Steak Tacos

Cooking time: 10 minutes

Portions: 12 persons

Ingredients:

- 2 lbs. flank steaks
- 1 tbsp. meat seasoning
- 1 lime juiced & 1 tsp. cuminutes
- ½ Tsp. salt & ground pepper
- 2 tbsp. minutesced garlic & 1 dash cayenne pepper
- ½ tsp. chili powder
- 2 tbsp. fresh cilantro

Directions:

1. Cut the fat from the meat if needed, then place it into a large bag together with the lime, 2 tbsp. of water, seasonings and place it in the fridge so everything will coat well.
2. Take out the meat and grill it for 5 minutes over each side. Start preparing the tortillas, adding the vegetables, grilled meat, and some seasonings.

Nutrition Facts:

1 portion: 134.8 calories, 6.7 g fat, 42.2 mg cholesterol, 160.1 mg sodium, 1.3 g carbs, 0.4 g dietary fiber, 16.4 g protein.

Chapter 3 – Fish and seafood

Honey-Cilantro Shrimp Soft Tacos

Cooking time: 25 minutes
Portions: 4 persons

Ingredients:

- 8 tortillas
- 1 tsp. vegetable oil
- ½ tbsp. salt and pepper
- 1 large onion & 1 jalapeno
- 3 bell peppers
- 2 tsp. coriander & cuminutes
- 2-4 garlic cloves
- 4 tbsp. fresh cilantro & honey
- 1 ½ lbs. cocktail shrimp

Directions:

1. Cook the shrimps, jalapeno, onion, bell peppers, seasonings and garlic into a medium skillet until they get tender. Into a glass bowl, combine the fresh cilantro and honey, until a smooth mixture is formed. Spoon the mixture over each tortilla; add the shrimps and some salsa sauce.

Nutrition Facts:

1 portion: 468.3 calories, 8.1 g fat, 331.9 mg cholesterol, 655.5 mg sodium, 57.3 g carbs, 3.2 g dietary fiber, 41.3 g protein.

Baja Fish Tacos

Cooking time: 20 minutes
Portions: 4 persons

Ingredients:

- 1 ½ lbs. thawed fresh tilapia filets
- 4 medium whole wheat tortillas
- 1 tbsp. fresh cilantro
- 1 onion, avocado and tomato (all chopped)
- 2 tsp. taco seasonings
- 2 cups cabbage slaw
- 1 lemon (juice)

Directions:

1. Finely chop the vegetables and shred the cabbage into small pieces. After seasoning the tilapia filets with taco seasoning, cook them into an oiled nonstick pan for 5-6 minutes.
2. Slowly cook the fish on both sides and add some onions, lemon juice, and tomatoes over. Warm each tortilla for 1 minute in the microwave, then add the fish filets, vegetables, cabbage, cilantro, and salsa.

Nutrition Facts:

1 portion: 366.8 calories, 12.7 g fat, 57.2 mg cholesterol, 426.3 mg sodium, 34.1 g carbs, 8.9 g dietary fiber, 30.8 g protein.

Shrimp Tacos

Cooking time: 30 minutes

Portions: 5 persons

Ingredients:

- 1 lb. peeled shrimp
- 10 corn tortillas
- ½ cup sour cream
- 1 tbsp. seasonings & 1 chipotle pepper
- 2 limes (for juice)
- ½ cup chopped purple cabbage
- 2 tbsp. virgin olive oil

Directions:

1. Combine the chipotle, half the lime juice and sour cream into a small bowl until a smooth paste gets formed. Into a preheated skillet start, cook the peeled shrimps with some seasonings. Warm up each taco and serve them topped with shredded cabbage, chipotle cream, fried shrimps, and sauce.

Nutrition Facts:

1 portion: 272.2 calories, 8.3 g fat, 148.8 mg cholesterol, 653.6 mg sodium, 27.2 g carbs, 4.7 g dietary fiber, 21.4 g protein.

Fish Tacos with Cilantro Slaw and Chipotle Mayo

Cooking time: 20 minutes
Portions: 4 persons

Ingredients:

- 1 pound tilapia fish fillets
- 4 flour tortillas
- $\frac{1}{2}$ cup fresh lime juice
- 2 cups 3-color coleslaw blend
- $\frac{1}{4}$ cup mayonnaise
- 1 chipotle chilies soaked in adobo sauce
- 1 cup minutesced fresh cilantro leaves
- 1 avocado & 1 diced tomato
- 1 tbsp. adobo sauce from chipotle peppers
- $\frac{1}{4}$ tsp. salt & cayenne pepper
- salt and ground black pepper

Directions:

1. Pour the lime juice over each tilapia fish filets and keep them into the refrigerator for 4 hours. Start preparing the chipotle mayonnaise dressing by mixing the adobo sauce, cayenne pepper, chilies, $\frac{1}{4}$ tsp. salt and mayonnaise into a medium bowl, mixing everything.
2. Take the fish out from the fridge and sauté it for 2-3 minutes into an oiled medium pan. Spread 1 tbsp. of chipotle sauce over each tortilla, add the cooked fish, veggies, and seasonings.

Nutrition Facts:

1 portion: 320.8 calories, 9.2 g fat, 60.7 mg cholesterol, 562.8 mg sodium, 33.6 g carbs, 5.8 g dietary fiber, 26.4 g protein.

Grilled Shrimp and Black Bean Tacos

Cooking time: 20 minutes
Portions: 6 persons

Ingredients:

- 1 lb. Peeled shrimp
- 12 corn tortillas
- 2 tbsp. chili powder
- 1 ½ tbsp. squeezed lime juice
- 1 cup black beans
- Pico de Gallo
- ½ Tsp. virgin olive oil
- ¼ tsp. salt
- 6 Skewers

Directions:

1. Preheat your grill, then prepare the sauce, heating up the black beans, lime juice, chili powder and salt into a medium pan. When a smooth paste is formed, prepare the shrimp skewers. They need to be fried for about 1-2 minutes for both sides, then brush each shrimp and grill them for another 2 minutes. Build your tortilla, adding the shrimps, sauce and seasonings.

Nutrition Facts:

1 portion: 245.4 calories, 3.3 g fat, 114.5 mg cholesterol, 257.4 mg sodium, 33.9 g carbs, 6.0 g dietary fiber, 21.7 g protein.

Blackened Cabo Fish Tacos

Cooking time: 30 minutes
Portions: 4 persons

Ingredients:

- 1½ lbs. white fish & 8 oz. fish marinade
- 12 corn tortillas
- ¾ lb. Asian Slaw
- 9 tbsp. lime sour cream
- 4 oz. butter
- 7 tbsp. chipotle aioli
- 7 tbsp. Pico de Gallo
- 2 tbsp. black pepper spice
- Chipotle Aioli
- ¾ cup mayonnaise
- 1 tsp. lime juice
- 1 tbsp. mustard
- Kosher salt & ground black pepper
- 2 chipotle peppers

Directions:

1. Into a medium saucepan, start melting the unsalted butter, add the marinated white fish, sprinkle some black pepper spice and fry them for 2 minutes on both sides. Warm each tortilla over both sides, add the fried chicken, the chipotle aioli sauce, a few Pico de Gallo, some Asian slaw and some seasonings.

Nutrition Facts:

1 portion: 893.9 calories, 60.8 g fat, 143.6 mg cholesterol, 690.2 mg sodium, 37.1 g carbs, 5.8 g dietary fiber, 50.5 g protein.

Spicy Shrimp Tacos

Cooking time: 35 minutes

Portions: 2 persons

Ingredients:

- 4 low-carb tortillas
- 4 tbsp. mango salsa sauce
- 16 large shrimps
- 1 tbsp. fresh chopped cilantro
- 1 cup Romaine lettuce
- ½ cup cheddar cheese
- 4 tsp. chili sauce
- ½ cup sauteed onions & 1 lime juice

Directions:

1. Start with the shrimps by marinating and skewering them into the siracha sauce for 5 minutes. Turn on the grill and cook the onions for a few minutes, until well cooked. Lay down each tortilla and top with sour cream, shrimps, lettuce, shredded cheese, grilled onions and other seasonings.

Nutrition Facts:

1 portion: 372.4 calories, 14.7 g fat, 120.3 mg cholesterol, 1,135.0 mg sodium, 39.5 g carbs, 18.8 g dietary fiber, 38.9 g protein.

Tilapia Tacos

Cooking time: 30 minutes
Portions: 1 person

Ingredients:

- 1 lb. Tilapia fish filet
- 2 white corn tortillas
- $\frac{1}{2}$ sliced avocado
- $\frac{1}{4}$ tsp. olive oil
- 1 tomato
- 1 white onion
- 1 lime juice
- 1 handful of cilantro

Directions:

1. Into a heated oven start broiling the tortillas and tilapia fish filet on both sides, but season the fish with some olive oil, salt and pepper. Into a medium bowl, mix   the tomato, lime juice, onion and the seasonings. Place a nice layer of shredded fish over each tortilla, add the mixture from the bowl, sliced avocado, then place the remaining fish on the top.

Nutrition Facts:

1 portion: 335.2 calories, 15.5 g fat, 50.8 mg cholesterol, 81.4 mg sodium, 32.1 g carbs, 8.5 g dietary fiber, 24.8 g protein.

Mojito-Grilled Fish Tacos with Lime Slaw Topping

Cooking time: 55 minutes
Portions: 8 persons

Ingredients:

- 8 corn tortillas
- 2 tbsp. lime juice
- 2 tbsp. minced mint leaves
- 1 lb. firm white fish (halibut, snapper or cod)
- 1 tbsp. canola oil
- 1 fresh jalapeno chile
- $\frac{1}{2}$ Tsp. salt & 1 tsp. sugar

Lime Slaw
- 2 tbsp. minutest
- $\frac{1}{2}$ cup low-fat mayonnaise
- $1\frac{1}{2}$ cups shredded cabbage
- 1 tbsp. fresh lime juice

Directions:

1. Start combining the fish and marinade ingredients together, then place it into   the fridge for 3 minutes. When done, take the fish out and start grill it over both sides, until it gets nice and firm.
2. For preparing the lime slaw, add the cabbage, mayonnaise, lime juice and mint into a medium bowl, stirring everything well. Place the fish on each tortilla, add some slaw spoons and vegetables.

Nutrition Facts:

1 portion: 444.7 calories, 9.1 g fat, 130.8 mg cholesterol, 219.7 mg sodium, 0.2 g carbs, 0.7 g dietary fiber, 84.3 g protein.

Grilled fish tacos with cilantro sauce

Cooking time: 30 minutes
Portions: 2 persons

Ingredients:

Sauce
- ¼ cup green onions & cilantro
- 2 ½ tbsp. mayonnaise
- 3 tbsp. sour cream
- 2 limes (juice)
- ½ tsp. salt, pepper & 1 garlic clove

Fish
- 2 lbs. red snapper steaks
- 4 corn tortillas
- 2 ½ cans cabbage
- 1 tbsp. ground cuminutes & coriander
- ½ tsp. red pepper, paprika & garlic salt

Directions:

1. Start combining the cilantro sauce ingredients in a medium bowl, then set it aside. For the fish, season it with some garlic powder, cuminutes, paprika, coriander and red pepper, grilling it for 5 minutes on both sides. Once the fish is done, cut it lengthwise and place it on tortillas, add the cabbage and 1 tbsp. of cilantro sauce on top.

Nutrition Facts:

1 portion: 285.5 calories, 9.1 g fat, 61.7 mg cholesterol, 512.2 mg sodium, 35.1 g carbs, 7.6 g dietary fiber, 19.2 g protein.

Conclusion

If you are an enthusiast person that loves to taste different kinds of world cuisines, you will definitely love the Mexican kitchen, but especially the tacos because they are the most delicious dish from Mexico. When you say the word "Mexico", the first word that comes to your mind might be the tacos or burritos. Besides the great taste of the tacos, many people won't probably know about the following fun facts of tacos:

It's said that tacos are really old

It is not known exactly when the first taco was created and you can see on the internet so many debates on this subject. Many experts consider that the tacos were invented around 1000-500 B.C. At that time, it was an indispensable food from every house, they were even considering it as a replacement of the nowadays "bread".

However, the name of "taco/tortilla" came later on, during the 19th century when the name was firstly introduced in the United States southern land around 1905. It became popular in Mexico a little before, when they were served for minutes that were working in silver mines.

The real fact is that Americans eat a ton of tacos

According to a recent study, the American people eat about 4.5 billion of tacos every year. Not only that they love so much the tacos, but they also got a symbol of Taco Bell, which they visit almost once 11 days.

You must have seen the biggest taco ever!

The biggest taco in the world was made on 20.11.2011 in Queretaro, Mexico, and it was about 246 feet long, containing carnitas as the main filling.

There is even a taco day; National Taco Day

For those that don't know the national day of tacos is on 4th October and every year, all over the world, it is celebrated by people. So why don't you go out and celebrate with others?

You must be surprised to hear that the word taco means "Light Lunch"

The translation of the taco word means "light lunch", but nowadays people cannot resist them and they don't keep it so light.

Now, that you found those interesting facts about tacos, I hope that we spark your interest in trying them and share this stuff with your friends while eating tacos with them.

Your Gift

I wanted to show my appreciation that you support my work so I've put together a free gift for you.

http://bonusfreebook.org/

Just visit the link above to download it now.

I know you will love this gift.

If you like this book, you can see and buy my other books on this link:

ALL BOOKS MAYA CLARK HERE

Thank you for attention!

With love,

Maya Clark

Legal & Disclaimer

The information contained in this book and its contents is not designed to replace or take the place of any form of medical or professional advice; and is not meant to replace the need for independent medical, financial, legal or other professional advice or services, as may be required. The content and information in this book have been provided for educational and entertainment purposes only.

The content and information contained in this book have been compiled from sources deemed reliable, and it is accurate to the best of the Author's knowledge, information, and belief. However, the Author cannot guarantee its accuracy and validity and cannot be held liable for any errors and/or omissions. Further, changes are periodically made to this book as and when needed. Where appropriate and/or necessary, you must consult a professional (including but not limited to your doctor, attorney, financial advisor or such other professional advisor) before using any of the suggested remedies, techniques, or information in this book.

Upon using the contents and information contained in this book, you agree to hold harmless the Author from and against any damages, costs, and expenses, including any legal fees potentially resulting from the application of any of the information provided by this book. This disclaimer applies to any loss, damages or injury caused by the use and application, whether directly or indirectly, of any advice or information presented, whether for breach of contract, tort, negligence, personal injury, criminal intent, or under any other cause of action.

You agree to accept all risks of using the information presented in this book.

You agree that by continuing to read this book, where appropriate and/or necessary, you shall consult a professional (including but not limited to your doctor, attorney, or financial advisor or such other advisor as needed) before using any of the suggested remedies, techniques, or information in this book.

18947444R00024

Made in the USA
Middletown, DE
03 December 2018